Jewels in the Landscape

A Celebration of Louisiana's Wildflowers

by

KELSO WALKER

2nd Edition

Library of Congress Catalog Number: 2001132979
ISBN Number: 1-887366-42-3

Printed in Canada

To my wife, best friend and helpmeet

Dianne Jennings Walker

"When a place is so lovely
I walk slow. I long to let loveliness drown in my soul.
I like to touch bird-feathers.
I blow deep into them to find the soft hairs beneath.
I like to count stamens, too
And even weigh their pollen-gold. The grass is a delight to sit on.
I do not need wine here because the flowers intoxicate me so ...."

Tu Fu, Chinest poet of the Tang Dynasty

"The invariable mark of wisdom is to see the miraculous in the common."

Ralph Waldo Emerson, from "Nature"

"Consider the lilies of the field, how they grow; they toil not, neither do
they spin: and yet I say to you, that even Solomon in all his glory was not
arrayed like one of these."

Jesus Christ

"1 shall return with the violets in spring. "

Napoleon, as he was being exiled to Elba

CONTENTS

PREFACE

I am not a botanist; I am a photographer and writer. A botanist did check my accuracy in identifying the wildflowers.

HOW TO USE THIS BOOK: The wildflowers in this book are arranged by color, beginning with red and ending with purplish-pink. This is roughly in accordance with the visible light spectrum (the colors you see when you allow sunlight to pass through a prism), or the colors of the rainbow. White flowers will be found between the yellow and green flowers. Some plants produce flowers in more than one color; in those cases I have attempted to include the most common color of the flower. In addition, many wildflowers are variable in color, say from white to pink or from pink to purple; therefore, if you do not find a flower in the appropriate color section, try another part of the book.

Under each photograph is the principal common name of the flower, and an X with a number, indicating the size of the picture relative to the actual size of the flower. For example, X 2 1/2 means the photograph is 2 1/2 times life size, X 1 means the photograph is life-size; and X 1/2 means the photograph is half life-size.

The scientific, or botanical, name is given next. This consists of two parts, in Latin (or the Latinized form of another language): first the genus, then the specific epithet. The genus and specific epithet is applied to a species, which is a group of similar plants.

No two plants have the same scientific name. Some wildflowers have many common names, and often the same common name refers to several different plants. What is a buttercup? For these reasons, it is useful to become familiar with the scientific names. These names are also interesting, often telling us something descriptive of the plant, so T have provided translations of many of the botanical names in this book.

Genera (the plural of genus) that share common characteristics are placed in the same family. For each wildflower I have given the family to which it belongs. Information about the family also appears in the text under some flowers.

Under the family name is the principal bloom period for the pictured flower. The actual period a wildflower is in blossom is not determined by the calendar, but by such factors as the amount of rainfall, sunshine and heat. Many wildflowers have occasional blossoms most of the year. These scattered blossoms are usually smaller than those of the principal blooming season.

The habitat of the pictured flower is given next. This tells you where you are most likely to find it; for example: roadsides, pine woods, prairies, marshes or seashore. If the wildflower only grows in part of the state, for example, north Louisiana, that information is also given.

WHAT IS A FLOWER? (See the illustration following the PREFACE) In addition to being a joy to behold, a flower is also the reproductive part of the plant. Its function is to produce a fruit and seeds, so that new plants may grow. The male reproductive organ is called the stamen, and consists of a filament topped by the anther, which contains the pollen grains. The female reproductive organ is called the pistil; its parts are stigma, style, and ovary. In order for fertilization to take place, for fruit and seeds to be produced, pollen must travel from the anther to the stigma, which is usually sticky; this is called pollination. Fertilization occurs in the swollen base of the pistil, the ovary, which contains the ovules, or embryonic seeds.

The other parts of a flower are the petals, which we all know, and the sepals, a circle of green, leafshaped parts outside the flower that enclose and protect it while in bud form. The petals are attractive not only to us, but also to insects, which aid pollination by brushing against the anther and stigma in turn, thereby transferring pollen grains.

A flower that has all of the above parts is called a complete flower. If any of the parts is missing, it is an incomplete flower. In the sunflower family, what we commonly think of as a flower is really a composite group of flowers, what a botanist would call a head. A typical sunflower has both disk and ray flowers, but there are exceptions.

WILDFLOWERS AND WEEDS: Any author of a book on wildflowers is bound to be asked the question, "What is the difference between a weed and a wildflower?" Actually, there is no difference between a flowering weed and a wildflower; the difference is in our perception. If we perceive a flower as a nuisance, we are likely to call it a weed, otherwise a wildflower. Some of our native orchids would be considered weeds if growing in a vegetable garden; bitterweeds growing along the highway may reasonably be considered wildflowers.

SEEING LOUISIANA'S WILDFLOWERS: From our northern piney woods to our sandy beaches on the Gulf of Mexico, Louisiana has an abundance of wildflowers. Some of these-not many-you may see while driving down the interstate at 70 miles per hour. You will see more wildflowers if you drive on a secondary road, especially if the right-of-way is not regularly mowed. But the best way to see wildflowers is to get out of your car and walk. Short walks (or in some cases wades) will bring you to most of the wildflowers featured in this book. Do not pick wildflowers, or dig them up.

Some of the wildflowers in this book are endangered species in Louisiana, and others are likely to become so, as human population pressures, herbicides, mowing, and paving continue. We must protect our abundant, beautiful, and diverse wildflowers if future generations are to enjoy them.

ABOUT THE PHOTOGRAPHS: All of the photographs in this book were taken by the author in the natural habitat of each wildflower. I used a medium format camera with Ektachrome and Kodachrome film. Natural lighting was used whenever possible; an electronic flash was used only as a last resort.

ACKNOWLEDGMENTS

I wish to thank the following people for their help at various stages in the development of this book: Charles Allen, Blair Bolles, Beth Erwin, Terry Erwin, Nelwyn Gilmore, Larry Raymond, Jay Richard, Rosaleen Richard, Jim Robbins, Julia Sanders, Jason Sonnier, Maxie Sonnier, Dale Thomas, Betty Torbert, John Torbert.

ABBREVIATIONS

sp. = species

spp. = species, plural

var. = variety

THE PARTS OF A FLOWER

Petal

Stamen

Pistil

PINK EVENING PRIMROSE
(a complete flower)

Disk Flowers

Ray Flowers

SUNFLOWER
(a composite flower)

Jewels in the Landscape

A Celebration of Louisiana's Wildflowers

CYPRESS VINE   X 1 1/8
Ipomoea quamoclit

FAMILY–Morning-glory (*Convolvulaceae*)
BLOOMS–June to frost
HABITAT–Fields, roadsides

    Ipomoea comes from two Greek words, *ips*, bind-weed; *homoios*, similar to. It entwines itself in surrounding vegetation. The leaf segments are thread-like and reminiscent of cypress needles. With its star-shaped red flower, this is possibly the prettiest member of the morning-glory family. It is an escaped exotic, tropical in origin.

CARDINAL FLOWER   X 1/4
Lobelia cardinalis

FAMILY–Bluebell (*Campanulaceae*)
BLOOMS–September to frost
HABITAT–Wet sites, swamps, stream banks; not commn

     This is the ony species of lobelia with red flowers. One tribe of American Indians ground up the dsried petals and threw them into the air, in order to stop approaching storms. White settlers made a de-worming medicine from the cardinal flower; all parts of this plant are poisonous. Hummingbirds visit it for its nectar.

CRIMSON CLOVER   X 1
Trifolium incarnatum

FAMILY–Pea (*Fabaceae*)
BLOOMS–March to June
HABITAT–Roadsides, waste areas, old fields

Probably the showiest of our roadside clovers, this is a native of Europe. It is cultivated for pasture, hay and, of course, soil improvement. The flowers have short, stiff hairs which can contribute to the formation of "hair balls" in the stomachs and intestines of horses, if ingested.

CORAL BEAN   X 3/8
Erythrina herbaceae

FAMILY–Pea (*Fabaceae*)
BLOOMS–April to June
HABITAT–Sandy, open woods, mostly pine forests

    Mamou is another name for this plant. It is a striking member of the vast pea family, not only for its spike of slender red flowers, but for its fruit, a pod of shiny scarlet beans. These beans were used for necklaces by the Native Americans; they are quite poisonous. The beans and roots were reported to be used gto make Mamou cough syrup.

CORAL HONEYSUCKLE   X 1 1/4
Lonicera sempervirens

FAMIILY–Honeysuckle (*Caprifoliaceae*)
BLOOMS–March to November
HABITAT–Woods, fence rows; widely distributed

     Although it twines around other plants, this beautiful native flower is not as agressive or abundant as the Japanese honeysuckle. Another common name for this plant is trumpet honeysuckle, referring to the shape of the individual flowers. The genus is named for Adam Lonicer, a sixteenth century German botanist.

RED PENTSTEMON   X 5/8
Penstemon murrayanus

FAMILY- Snapdragon (*Scrophulariaceae*)
BLOOMS-April to June
Habitat-Dry, sandy soil

This rare beauty, which is found only in east Texas and northwestern Louisiana, is a critically endangered species. It is named for Johann Andreas Murray, an 18th century Swedish professor of botany and medicine, who studied under Linnaeus.

RED BUCKEYE   X 3/8
Aesculus pavia

FAMILY-Horse chestnut (*Hippocastanaceae*)
BLOOMS-March to May
Habitat-Along streams, especially in hilly areas

     Red Buckeye is usually a large shrub, but it occasionally reaches tree size. The "buckeye" is the large seed, which contains a white scar from the point of attachment to its capsule. These seeds are poisonous; they are carried in the pockets of some people to keep rheumatism away.

TRUMPET CREEPER   X 1 1/8
Campsis radicans

FAMILY-Bignonia (*Bignoniaceae*)
BLOOMS-May to November
HABITAT-Climbs on trees, fences; widespread

This high-climbing woody vine has showy flowers that range from orange to red. It creeps to the tops of tall trees using aerial roots (*radicans* means having rooting stems). Contact with the leaves and flowers may cause dermatitis in some people; cow-itch is one of its common names. Hummingbirds are attracted to the flowers.

RED IRIS   X 7/8
Iris fulva

FAMILY–*Iris (Iridaceae}*
BLOOMS–March to May
HABITAT–Marshes, swamps, wet areas

When this iris was found growing near New Orleans in 1811, it created something of a sensation–it was gthe first red iris discovered. The flower has an almost flat form, and is smaller than most irises. The color varies from red to salmon pink. *Fulva* means tawny-orange. Another name for this lovely flower is copper iris.

TRILLIUM   X 3/8
Trillium ludovicianum

FAMILY–Lily (Liliaceae)
BLOOMS–March to May
HABITAT–Shady, moist woods

    Trillium comes from the Latin word for three, a reference to the fact that the plant has three sepals, petals, etc. The common name wake robin alludes to its early spring blooming period. The root was used by Indians to ease childbirth, giving rise to another common name, birthroot. *Ludvicianum* means of Louisiana (or the Louisiana Purchase territory).

BUTTERFLY-WEED   X 3/4

Asclepias tuberosa

FAMILY–Milkweed (Asclepiadaceae)
BLOOMS– May to July
HABITAT–Sandy, upland soil

This prettiest of milkweeds is one of two species lacking the typical milky sap, or latex. It is called butterfly-weed because butterflies are attracted to it, especially the monarch, whose larvae use the plant as a food source. The root has been used to make a tea for treating cough, whence another common name, pleurisy-root. It is also called orange milkweed.

CAROLINA LILY   X 7/8
Lilium michauxii

FAMILY–Lily (*Liliaceae*)
BLOOMS–July to August
HABITAT–Rich woods, pine-hardwood areas of west and southeast Louisiana

     Carolina Lily is not common in Louisiana, and many plants do not flower every year. The blossoms (1, occasionally 2 or 3) hang gracefully from curved stalks. The leaves, which grow in circles around the lower stem, are widest near the tip. The plant reaches a maximum height of about four feet.

YELLOW–FRINGED ORCHID   X 7/8
Habenaria ciliaris

FAMILY–Orchid (*Orchidaceae*)
BLOOMS–July to September
HABITAT– Moist pinelands and bogs

     This is simply one of the most beautiful wildflowers in America. The effect upon one of suddenly finding a group of these golden-fringed beauties is overwhelming. They reach a height of about forty inches. *Habenaria* comes from the Latin word for rein, possibly referring to the strap-shaped fringed (*ciliaris*) lip.

TICKSEED   X 1
Coreopsis lanceolata

FAMILY–Sunflower (*Asteraceae*)
BLOOMS–March to June
HABITAT–Dry soil in pinewoods, prairies, roadsides

     If you are in one of the above habitats in spring, you can'tmiss the roadside colonies of these lovely flowers. *Coreopsis* (also a common name for this plant) means bug-like, a reference to its seeds, which resemble a small bug or tick. The flower heads can produce a yellow dye suitable for wool.

YELLOW TOP   X 1 1/8
Senecio glabellus

FAMILY–Sunflower (*Asteraceae*)
BLOOMS–December to May
HABITAT–Fields, pastures, roadsides; widespread and abundant

    In late winter and early spring, yellow tops blanket pastures and fallow fields by the acre–a cheerful site at that time of year. This and other members of the genus *Senecio* are suspected of being poisonous to cattle. This plant is also known by the common name butterweed.

SEASIDE GOLDENROD   X 5/8
Solidago sempervirens var. Mexicana

FAMILY–Sunflower (*Asteraceae*)
BLOOMS–August to November
HABITAT–Gulf coast, wet places near coast

    Most goldenrods are next to impossible to identify, since the species are so numerous, similar , and variable. We may call the lovely flower shown above *Soidago sempervirens* var. *Mexicana* because of its habitat, succulent leaves and single golden "rod". It grows to a height of siX feet.

NARROW-LEAVED SUNFLOWER   X 3/4
Helianthus angustifolius

FAMILY–Sunflower (*Asteraceae*)
BLOOMS–August to November
HABITAT–Moist ground, widely distributed

Ths sunflower may be identified by its dark disk flowers at the tips of slender branches of a single stem; and by its narrow leaves, which are only one-sixteenth to one-fourth inch wide. The plant may reach a height of seven feet. Wild sunflower seeds are a food source for many kinds of birds. *Helianthus angustifolia* means narrow-leaved sunflower.

BLACK-EYED SUSAN   X 7/8
Rudbeckia hirta

FAMILY–Sunflower (*Asteraceae*)
BLOOMS–April to August
HABITAT-Woodlands, old fields, roadsides; common

    The genus *Rudbeckia* is named for a pair of early Swedish botanists, father and son, both named Olaf Rudbeck. *Hirta* means hairy or shaggy. This attractive roadside flower sometimes covers whole fields. The upper one-third of the stem has no leaves. This is the state flower of Maryland.

INDIAN BLANKET   X 1 1/8
Gaillardia aestivalis

FAMILY–Sunflower (*Asrteraceae*)
BLOOMS–May to October
HABITAT–Prairies, pinelands

    Though perhaps not as showy as the Indian blanket (*Gaillardia pulchella*) commonly planted along our highways, this is nonetheless, a very attractive wildflower. The three-lobed yellow ray flowers are sometimes absent. The plant, which is covered with stiff hairs, is about two feet tall. *Aestivalis* is from the Latin word for summer, reflecting this flower's main blooming season.

PUCCOON   X 3/4
Lithospermum caroliniese

FAMILY–Borage (*Boraginaceae*)
BLOOMS–March to May
HABITAT–Dry, sandy pinewoods

    The flowers of this genus produce white, stony seeds, hence the name *Lithispermum* or stone-seed. Puccoon is from the Algonquin Indian name for these flowers. The roots of this plant were used by Indians to make a red-purple dye; the leaves are narrow and hairy. Forget-me nots are also in the borage family.

INDIAN STRAWBERRY   X 3 1/2
Duchesnea indica

FAMILY– Rose (*Rosaceae*)
BLOOMS–April to August
HABITAT-Moist ground all over the eastern United States

    This is *not* a wild strawberry, although the leaves and fruit resemble one. A native of Asia, it has escaped into our lawns and waste areas. The red fruit–though inviting– is virtually tasteless. The real wild strawberry, *Fragaria virginia* is white-flowered, and found only in Bossier, St Helena, St Tammany and Washington parishes, where it may have escaped from cultivation.

BITTERWEED   X 1/2
Helenium amarum

FAMILY–Sunflower (*Asteraceae*)
BLOOMS-June to frost
HABITAT–Roadsides, dry areas, fields, pastures, waste areas

     If you have tasteds the milk of cows that have grazed this plant then you do not need to told the origin of the common name. And yet– with its delicate, lacy leaves and yellow flowers–it is a pretty plant. *Helenium* is from the Greek name for another plant which sprang from the tears of Helen of Troy, according to Pliny the Elder (23-79 A.D.); *amarum* is Latin for bitter.

COMPASS PLANT   X 3/4
Silphium gracile

FAMILY–Sunflower (*Asteraceae*)
BLOOMS-April to July
HABITAT-Prairies, longleaf pinelands

   Unlike most other sunflowers, members of the *Silphium* genus have ray flowers that produce seeds, and disk flowers that do not. These coarse plants have large, usually yellow flower heads, and produce a sticky resin, or rosin, on the stems and leaves of which are said to point north and south if the leaves are erect. Rosin weed is another common name for this plant. *S. gracile* reaches a height of three or more feet.

GOLDENROD   X 1/2
Solidago canadensis

FAMILY–Sunflower (*Asteraceae*)
BLOOMS-August
HABITAT–Roadsides, pastures, idle land; common throughout Louisiana

      There is no proof that these flowers cause " hay fever"; ragweed is the more likely villain. If you don't believe that goldenrods are members of the sunflower family, look more closely. You will see numerous tiny flower heads with both dfisk and ray flowers. Another species of goldenrod, *Soidago gigantea* is the state flower of Kentucky and Nebraska

DANDELION   X 3/8
Taraxacum officinale

FAMILY–Sunflower (*Asteraceae*)
BLOOMS–February to June; scattered blossoms nearly all year
HABITAT–Lawns, grassy, open areas; almost everywhere in the U.S.

Consider these facts about the lowly dandelion: the seeds are eaten by songbirds; the vitamin-rich young leaves are edible in salads, or cooked as a potherb; the flowers produce a golden wine; the nectar is gathered by bees for making honey; and a drug used for treating the liver is obtained from the root. Do you still consider this plant a weed?

CLASPING-LEAF CONEFLOWER   X 1
Dracopis amplexicaule

FAMILY–Sunflower (*Asteraceae*)
BLOOMS–April to July
HABITAT–Roadsides

    This lovely roadside flower can be easily distinguished from the black-eyed susan by its tall disk, or cone, and by its leaves, which clasp the stem. *Amplexicaule* means stem-embracing. This plant reaches a height of about five feet.

CONE-FLOWER   X 1/2
Rudbeckia nitida var. texana

FAMILY– SUNFLOWER (*Asteraceae*)
BLOOMS–June to July
HABITAT–Moist prairies, pinelands

   The broad leaves of this tall coneflower are all at the base of the stem. The common name refers to the cone-shaped disk. *Nitida* means shining, probably an allusion to the bright yellow rays, which slope downward. The plant grows to a height of about five feet.

PARTRIDGE PEA   X 5/8
Cassia fasciculate

FAMILY–Pea (*Fabaceae*)
BLOOMS–June to October
HABITAT–Sandy, open places, sunny spots, roadsides

     This flower has five unequal petals: the three upper petals have a maroon spot at the base; one of the lower petals is cupped, the other much broader and flatter. The larva of the sulphur butterfly feeds on the leaves; the seeds are eaten by quail. Another name for this plant is prairie senna.

COREOPSIS   X 1 1/8
Coreopsis tinctoria

FAMILY–Sunflower (Asteraceae)
BLOOMS–May to June
HABITAT–Roadsides, disturbed soils

     With its maroon blotches at the base of its yellow disk flowers, this is one of our most striking wildflowers. *Tinctoria* derives from the Latin word meaning to dye, and indeed a red dye can be obtained from this plant. It may grow as high as five feet.

INDIAN BLANKET   X 7/8
Gaillardia pulchella

FAMILY–Sunflower (*Asteraceae*)
BLOOMS–April to frost
HABITAT–Sand soil along the gulf coast; widely planted along roadsides

     This flower is extremely variable, the rays being red or maroon to purple, and usually tipped with yellow. This mixture of colors resembles the colors found in Indian blankets. Another common name is firewheel. Galliard was a French botany patron; *pulchella* means pretty.

SUNFLOWER   X 3/8
Helianthus mollis

FAMILY–Sunflower(*Asteraceae*)
BLOOMS–June to September
HABITAT–Prairies, pinelands

Arguably the most beautiful of our wild sunflowers, *Helianthus mollis* is characterized by a dense covering of soft, white hairs on the stem and leaves (*mollis* means soft). The leaves are egg-shaped and clasp the stem. Although it may reach the towering height of eight feet, this plant is commonly under four feet.

YELLOW JESSAMINE   X 1 3/8
Gelsemium sempervirens

FAMILY–Logania (*Loganiaceae*)
BLOOMS–January to April
HABITAT–Climbs on trees; widespread

I have had the experience of seeing, in the distance, a tree with yellow flowers, only to discover when I got closer that the tree was covered with yellow Jessamine. The sweet-smelling flowers, leaves and roots of this woody vine are poisonous, and can cause death due to respiratory failure. Yellow Jessamine, also known as false jessamine, is the state flower of South Carolina.

YELLOW FLAG   X 1/2
Iris pseudacorus

FAMILY–Iris (*Iridaceae*)
BLOOMS–April to May
HABITAT–Wet, open spaces; all over, especially south Louisiana

    This beautiful Iris is an escaped exotic originating in Europe and growing wild from Newfoundland to Louisiana. The sepals are marked with dark lines and dots. The underground stem yields a black dye. Yellow flag grows to about five feet high.

YELLOW WOOD SORREL   X 1 1/4
Oxalis srtricta

FAMILY–Wood sorrel (*Oxalidaceae*)
BLOOMS–March to May
HABITAT–Fallow fields, lawns, waste places

      This is the most common yellow wood sorrel in Louisiana. The term oxalic acid comes from the name of this plant. *Oxalis*, meaning sour or acid. *Stricta* means erect, and refers to the growing habit of the plant, which is about a foot tall. The leaves are toxic in large quantities; children should not be allowed to chew them. Another common name for this plant is sour grass.

FALSE DANDELION   X 7/8

Pyrrhoppus carolinianus

FAMILY–Sunflower (*Asteraceae*)
BLOOMS–April to July
HABITAT–Open fields, lawns, woodlands; widespread and abundant

Easily and commonly mistaken for a dandelion, ths plant is taller and prettier. It has only ray flowers. The flower opens in the morning and is closed by early afternoon. Like the true dandelion, the false dandelion has a globular seed-head, whose seeds are scattered hither and yon by the wind–or by blowing and making a wish.

COLIC-ROOT   X 3/4
Aletris aurea

FAMILY–Lily (*Liliaceae*)
BLOOMS–May to July
HABITAT-Pinelands, prairies

    The bitter roots of these slender, striking plants were once used as a treatment for colic and other ailments. Other common names are star-grass and yellow star-grass. See the yellow star-grass on page 41 for an example of the unreliability of common names. *Aurea* means gold.

DRUMMOND'S EVENING PRIMROSE   X 5/8
Oenothera drummondii

FAMILY–Evening primrose (*Onagraceae*)
BLOOMS-April to June
HABITAT-Sandy beaches of the gulf coast

In the late afternoon the flower opens and turns toward the sun, closing the next morning. This hairy, sprawling plant is native to our coast. It is also known by the name beach evening primrose.

ST. JOHN'S WORT   X 7/8
Hypericum sp.

FAMILY–St. John's-wort (*Hypericaceae*)
BLOOMS-June to September
HABITAT–Prairies, pinelands

No wildflower has had more magical powers attributed to it than this one. It is in bloom on June 24th (St John's Day or Midsummer Day). In antiquity, if you hung St. John's-wort over your door on St. John's Eve you would be protected from demons, ghosts, thunderbolts and all manner of illness.

YELLOW STAR-GRASS   X 3 1/2
Hypoxis hirsuta

FAMILY–Amaryllis (*Amaryllidaceae*)
BLOOMS–February to April
HABITAT–Dry, sandy land, esp. pinelands, open woodlands, meadows

    This species is aptly named, for both the flowers and grass-like leaves are very hirsute, or hairy. The stems rise only a few inches from the ground, and are capped by one, or few, beautiful six-pointed stars. The leaves are up to eighteen inches long. The flowers are a good source of pollen and nectar in early spring.

DOLLAR-WEED   X 7/8
Rhynchosia reniformis

FAMILY–Pea (*Fabaceae*)
BLOOMS–May to September
HABITAT–Sandy soil in pinelands

    Rhnchosia (from Greek) refers to the beak shape of the keel , or lower two petals. *Reniformis* menas kidney-shaped, an allusion to the leaves, which are one to a leaf-stalk. This little plant is erect and reaches a height of eight inches. Other members of this genus are vines.

EVENING PRIMROSE   X 1 1/8
Oenothera biennis

FAMILY–Evening primrose (*Onagraceae*)
BLOOMS–April to frost
HABITAT–Dry fields, pastures, other open areas; widely distributed

At least on person has claimed he can *hear* these flowers open on a summer evening. Whether you can hear them or not, their creamy yellow blossoms are a delight as they unfurl at twilight time. This species reaches a height of siX to seven feet.

YELLOW POLYGALA   X 3/4
Polygala ramose

FAMILY–Milkwort (*Polygalaceae*)
BLOOMS–April to September
HABITAT–Wet, sandy pinelands

     Certainly one of the showiest of the *polygalas*, this species has a branched (*ramose*) cluster of flowers up to siX inches across. The plant is up to twenty inches tall. The *gala* (milk) in *polygala* is the same *gala* found in the word galaxy, e.g., our milky way.

PENCIL FLOWER   X 7/8
Stylosanthes biflora

FAMILY–Pea (*Fabaceae*)
BLOOMS–May to September
HABITAT–Pinelands, prairies, thin, dry woods; widely disrributed

    This little yellow legume has a pencil-like hollow tube to which the petals are attached. The botanical name (from Greek *stylos,* column, *anthos*, flower) also refers to this structure. The leaves are divided into three leaflets. This plant is usually erect, and grows to a height of two feet.

SOW-THISTLE   X 1
Sonchus asper

FAMILY–Sunflower (*Asteraceae*)
BLOOMS-December to June
HABITAT–Lawns, disturbed soils, fields

    This European native has escaped to our city streets, as well as our country farms. The small flower heads consist of all ray flowers. Birds eat the seeds. The spine-edged leaves are coarse and unattractive. The plant, which contains a milky sap, is usually about two feet tall. *Sonchus* is the Greek name for sow-thistle; *asper* means rough.

PRICKLY PEAR   X 3/4
Opuntia humifusa

FAMILY–Cactus (*Cactaceae*)
BLOOMS–May to June
HABITAT–Dry, sandy, open woods

    Yes we have cacti in Louisiana–three species , in fact. This one is low-growing, armed with spines, and its joints are easily broken off. The reddish fruit has been used for food in the southwestern U.S. and Mexico. Many cacti have escaped from cultivation, but they may have been native to west Louisiana. *Humifusa* means sprawling on the ground.

PRIMROSE–WILLOW   X 1 1/8
Ludwigia decurrens

FAMILY–Evening primrose (*Onagraceae*)
BLOOMS–June to October
HABITAT–Swamps, shallow water, wet places

The flower looks like a primrose, and the leaves resemble those of the willow, so we get the name primrose-willow. *Decurrens* means running down the stem, which the flanged bases of the leaves of this species do. The plant may reach a height of siX feet.

EARLY BUTTERCUP   X 3/8
Ranunculus fascicularis

FAMILY–Crowfoot (*Ranunculaceae*)
BLOOMS–March to April
HABITAT–Prairies, woods, open areas

     Buttercups are easily recognized by their shiny petals. This condition is caused by a special layer of cells just below the surface. Members of this genus contain the volatile oil protoanemonin, which causes blisters when touched. The leaves can cause severe inflammation of the intestinal tract of eaten without thorough cooking.

ST. PETER'S–WORT   X 1
Ascryum stans

FAMILY–Sr. John's-wort (*Hypericaceae*)
BLOOMS–June to Septermber
HABITAT–Sandy, upland soil, pinelands

St.Peter's–wort is easily distinguished from the more common St.John-wort by its four, rather than five yellow petals. This species is also characterized by its unusual sepals: two very broad, enclosing two very narrow ones. It is a small shrub, one to three feet tall, with oval leaves. *Ascyrum* means smooth; *stans* means erect. The suffiX "–wort" just means plant.

50

GROUND-CHERRY   X 7/8
Physalis viscosa

FAMILY–Nightshade (*Solanaceae*)
BLOOMS–March to October
HABITAT–Sandy areas near the Gulf of Mexico

    Physalis is from the Greek for bladder; the sepals of this flower gradually grow in size until they unite, forming the bladder, which surrounds the fruit or ground-cherry. *Viscosa* means sticky. This species is about a foot high, and is covered with soft hair. The fruit is poisonous when green, and not very edible when ripe.

EVENING PRIMROSE   X 1 1/8
Oenothera laciniata

FAMILY–Evening primrose (*Onagraceae*)
BLOOMS–March to October
HABITAT–Fields, gardens, waste places

     This small night-blooming plant reaches a height of two feet. The leaves are deeply cleft–that is the meaning of *laciniata*. The genus name is from two Greek words: *oinos*, wine; *thera*, pursuing. The roots of these plants were thought to increase one's capacity for wine.

NODDING INDIGO   X 5/8
Baptisia leucophaeae

FAMILY–Pea (*Fabaceae*)
BLOOMS–April to May
HABITAT–Sandy soil in prairies, pinelands

    This species of *Baptisia* is a low, wide-spreading, bushy plant. Its large flower clusters have the curious habit of drooping or "nodding", below the leaves, or actually on the ground. *Leucophaeae* means dusk-white, but the flowers range in color from white to yellow. Plains wild indigo and cream wild indigo are also common names for this plant.

ALUM-ROOT   X 3/8
Heuchera Americana

FAMILY–Saxifrage (*Saxifragaceae*)
BLOOMS–April to June
HABITAT–Rich north Louisiana woods

    This is a rare and endangered species in Louisiana. The tall flowering stem bears many minute flowers with protruding stamens. The large, broad leaves, which turn reddish in winter, are at he base of the plant. The common name derivers from the astringent quality of the underground stem (the substance alum is astringent).

LOUSEWORT   X 1 3/8
Pedicularis Canadensis

FAMILY-Snapdragon (*Scrophulariaceae*)
BLOOMS–March to May
HABITAT–Open, well drained pine-hardwood areas

    Long ago it was believed that livestock grazing on this plant would become infested with lice. *Pedicularis* is from the Latin word for louse. The flowers are in dense spikes; the color is yellow or greenish–yellow. The leaves resemble ferns. Fernleaf and wood-betony are other common names for this plant, which is somewhat dependent on the roots of other plants for nutrition.

CANDY ROOT   X 3/4
Polygala nana

FAMILY–Milkwort (*Polygalaceae*)
BLOOMS–April to October
HABITAT–Pinelands; widely distributed and cimmon

    These pretty little flowers are siX inches or less tall, and grow in little tufts. The name candy root is derived from the fact that children chewed the roots, which smell and taste like wintergreen candy. Another name for these flowers is bachelor's button.

YELLOW PITCHER-PLANT   X 7/8
Sarracacenia alata

FAMILY–Pictcher-plant (*Sarraceniaceae*)
BLOOMS–March to April
HABITAT–Bogs in southeast and southwest Louisiana

      Pitcher-plants have hollow leaves with downward-pointing hairs, which prevent insects from escaping. The trapped insects are digested by enzymes in the water at the base of the leaves, providing some of the plants' nutrition. There are no man-eating plants in Louisiana. Other common names are fly catcher, frog belly and yellow trumpets.

TEAWEED   X 1 1/8
Sida rhombifolia

FAMILY–Mallow (*Malvaceae*)
BLOOMS–April to October
HABITAT–Waste areas, roadsides, sidewalks, lawns

     I consider this plant a weed because it grows where it is not wanted–my yard. Because it has a very tough stem, a long, tough taproot, it is difficult to remove. The leaves are variable, but are usually diamond (rhomboid) shaped, whence the specific name. This plant may reach a height of four feet, in which case you are in trouble. It is also known as sida and false mallow.

OAK-LEAVED HYDRANGEA   X 1/8

Hydrangea quercifolia

FAMILY–Saxifrage (*saxifragaceae*)
BLOOMS–April to June
HABITAT–Rich woods on hills

     This shrub, which reaches a height of twelve feet, has an unusual flower arrangement; a cluster of sterile flowers with four petal-like bracts, mixed with tiny complete flowers. *Hydrangea* is from tow Greek words meaning water jar, a reference to the shape of the fruit. *Quercifolia* means oak-leaved.

AMERICAN LOTUS   X 1/8
Nelumbo lutea

FAMILY–Water-lotus (*Nelumbonaceae*)
BLOOMS–April to August
HABITAT–Ponds, lakes, slow-moving streans

  This beautiful, flamboyant aquatic plant is unmistakable. The round leaves, which are up to two feet in diameter, rise above the water. In the center of the flower is a cone with numerous holes on the upper surface. An edible seed develops inside each hole. The roots were cooked and eaten by the Indians. Other common names are lotus-lily and water chinquapin.

WOOLLY ROSE–MALLOW   X 3/4
Hibiscus lasiocarpos

FAMILY–Mallow (*Malvaceae*)
BLOOMS–May to September
HABITAT–Swamps, marshes, ditches, wet sites

The mallow family includes cultivated cotton and okra plants, as well as some of our most striking wildflowers. This species, which reaches a height of siX feet, has a purple-red center, and leaves that are velvety all over. *Lasiocarpos* means woolly-fruited, a reference to the hairy capsule-shaped seed pod. This flower also comes in pink.

JAPANESE HONEYSUCKLE   X 1
Lonicera japonica

FAMILY–Honeysuckle (*Caprifoliaceae*)
BLOOMS–March to frost
HABITAT–Superabundant in many places in Louisiana

This escaped exotic runs rampant over native and cultivated vegetation, fence rows, and anything else in its way. Then why do some people buy it and plant it as an ornamental? It must be the deliciously sweet smell of those pretty little flowers.

BUTTON–BUSH   X 3/8
Cephalanthus occidentalis

FAMILY–Madder (*Rubiaceae*)
BLOOMS–June to September
HABITAT–In, or on the edge of, water

The spherical flower clusters of this shrub resemble pins in pincushions. The fragrant flowers attract bees; the larva of the smeared dagger moth feeds on the leaves. The bark, which is poisonous, has been used medicinally to treat a variety of ailments. This plant is also known as button willow and honeyballs.

GOAT'S RUE   X 1 1/8
Tephrosia virginiana

FAMILY–Pea (*Fabaceae*)
BLOOMS–April to June
HABITAT–Dry, sandy pinelands

     This plant contains the natural insecticide rotenone. Small amounts of the substance were used medicinally by American Indians, as well as early settlers. Caribbeans used it to poison fish. Goat's rue, also known as rabbit's pea, hoary pea, devil's shoestring and catgut. It is easily recognized by its large, cream-colored and rose flowers and feathery leaves.

WHITE DUTCH CLOVER   X 1 1/8
Trifolium repens

FAMILY–Pea (*Fabaceae*)
BLOOMS–January to May. Scattered blossoms throughout the year
HABITAT–Lawns, pastures, open fields

The clover found in our lawns, this European native is a favorite of bees; it is the source of clover honey. Four-leafed clovers are considered good luck; if you find a five-leafed clover and keep it, it is considered bad luck–but if you give it away it is good luck to both people.

WHITE INDIGO   X 1/2
Baptisia lactea

FAMILY–Pea (*Fabaceae*)
BLOOMS–April to June
HABITAT–Prairies and pinelands

This striking legume reaches a height of five to siX feet. In spring it can cause poisoning of cattle; in summer the entire plant withers and turns black. *Baptisia* comes from a Greek word meaning to dye. Members of this genus have been used as a substitute for true indigo, *Indigofera*. *Lactea* means milk-colored.

MOUNTAIN-MINT   X 1/2
Pycnanthemium tenuifolium

FAMILY–Mint (*Lamiaceae*)
BLOOMS–May to September
HABITAT–Open, thin pine woods, prairies, roadsides; widely distributed

     If these flowers were appropriately named they would not be fpound in Louisiana, as we have no mountains. They have the typical square stem and minty odor of the mint family. *Pycnanthemum* means densely flowered; *tenuifolium* means delicately leaved.

WHITE WATER–LILY   X 1/4
Nymphaea odorata

FAMILY–Water-lily (*Nymphaeaceae*)
BLOOMS–April to July
HABITAT–Still, fresh water throughout the state

      Water-lilies are not related to the lily famly. The fragrant flowrers open in the morning and close in the afternoon, for several days in a row. The genus is named after Nymphe, on of the water-nymphs of Greek mythology. Other common names are fragrant water-lily and water-nymph.

ALLIGATOR WEED   X 1 1/4
Alternanthera philoxeroides

FAMILY–Amaranth (*Amaranthaceae*)
BLOOMS–April to October
HABITAT–Fresh water marshes, ditches

    An escaped exotic from South America, alligator weed is second only to water-hyacinth as a pest in our fresh water marshes. The horizontal stems, with upward-growing branches grow quickly, forming dense mats that can clog waterways. It is intolerant of salt water, and is therefore a good indicator of fresh water.

WILD SCABIOSA   X 5/8

Hymenopappas scabiosaeus

FAMILY–Sunflower (*Asteraceae*)
BLOOMS–April to June
HABITAT–Open, dry, sandy pinelands of north and west Louisiana

    This unusual wildflower resembles the cultivated pincushion flower, *Scabiosa atropurpurea,* but it is in a different genus. The stem and the underside of the leaves are covered with short, white hairs–perhaps effective against itching or scabies. Wild scabiosa is two to four feet tall.

FALSE GARLIC   X 1 1/4

Nothoscordom bivalve

FAMILY–Lily (*Liliaceae*)
BLOOMS–Late February to April
HABITAT–Fields, lawns, prairies

    Nothoscordum is simply Latin for false garlic. There is no garlic or onion odor present. These badly named flowers blanket whole fields in late winter, but are best seen up close, where they will be appreciated for what they are: jewel-like members of the lily family.

MAGNOLIA   X 3/8
Magnolia grandiflora

FAMILY–Magnolia (*Magnoliaceae*)
BLOOMS–April to June; scattered blossom to November
HABITAT–Rich bottomland, gentle-sloping , sandy upland soil

The state flower of both Louisiana and Mississippi, this native tree is widely planted as an ornamental. The flowers are up to nine inches across, and are perfectly white, unless bruised–which they always seem to be. The genus was named by Linnaeus for Pierre Magnol (1638–1751), director of the botanic garden at Montpellier, France.

YUCCA   X 1/8
Yucca louisianensis

FAMILY–Lily (*Liliaceae*)
BLOOMS–April to June
HABITAT–Dry, sandy hill areas

    Yucca is generally a western genus, but several species ae native to Louisiana. *Yucca louisianensis* has a rosette of long narrow leaves at its base, and a flowering stem siX to eight feet tall. The yucca moth plays an essential part in the reproductive cycle of these plants. Yucca is the state flower of New Mexico.

WHITE RAIN-LILY   X 3/4
Zephryanthes candida

FAMILY–Amaryllis (*Amaryllidaceae*)
BLOOMS–April to September
HABITAT–Low areas, waste areas

    This beautiful escaped exotic is from South America. Unlike other members of the *Zephranthes* genus, *Zephranthes candida* has one stigma with three lobes, instead of the usual three stigmas. The plant is about a foot high. Other common names are fall crocus, zephyr-lily and zephyr flower, from the Greek *zephyros,* the west wind.

SWAMP-LILY   X 3/8
Crinum americanum

FAMILY–Amaryllis (*Amaryllidaceae*)
BLOOMS–May to November
HABITAT–Fresh water marshes, swamps, ditches of south Louisiana

The pretty swamp-lily is distinguished from the spider-lily by the absence of the cup, oe crown, in the middle of the flower. These flowers, usually four per stem, are fragrant and have rose-colored stamens. *Crinum* is from the Greek *krynon*, meaning lily. Neither the swamp-lily nor the spider-lily is a true lily, both being in the Amaryllis family. Another name for this plant is string lily.

WHITE COLIC-ROOT   X 3/8
Aletris farinosa

FAMILY–Lily (*Liliaceae*)
BLOOMS–April to July
HABITAT–Flat, grassy pineland

     Aletris was a female Greek slave who ground grain. These flowers, as well as the yellow species, have a mealy (*farinosa*) appearance. The narrow spike of little cylindrical flowers stands about three feet tall. Other common names are millet's maid and white star grass.

WHITE PRAIRIE CLOVER   X 1 3/8
Petalostemum candidum

FAMILY–Pea (*Fabaceae*)
BLOOMS–May to June
HABITAT–Prairies, pinelands

    The petals and stamens are joined in this atypical member of the pea family, and this is reflected in the genus name, which is a combination of two Greek words meaning petal and stamen. *Candidum* is a Latin word meaning shiny-white. The flower cluster blossoms from the bottom up. The plant is one to two feet high.

WHITE GAURA   X 3/4
Gaura lindheimeri

FAMILY–Evening primrose (*Onagraceae*)
BLOOMS–April to September
HABITAT–Prairies, pinelands

     If you are among those who like to count stamens, this is the flower for you. The four irregular petals face upward; the long stamens and pistils droop downward. The late Caroline Dorman likened this wildflower to a small white butterfly. It is fragrant and attracts beds and other insects. *Gaura* means superb. The maximum height is about siX feet.

WILD BERGAMONT   X 1/2
Monarda lindheimeri

FAMILY–Mint (*Lamiaceae*)
BLOOMS–May to August
HABITAT–Dry soil in prairies, open woods

     This pleasantly fragrant member of the mint family is a favorite of bumblebees, hence the other common name, bee balm. Indians and early settlers made medicinal teas from the plant. The genus is named for Nicholas Monardes, a sixteenth century Spanish physician and botanical writer. Bergamont is sometimes spelled bergamot. The color of the fower may be white, pink or lavender.

HEDGE BINDWEED   X 3/4
Calystegia sepium

FAMILY–Morning-glory (*Convolvulaceae*)
BLOOMS–May to September
HABITAT–Fields, thickets, waste areas

Bindweeds have tow narrow stigmas at the tip of the style; morning-glories have single round stigma. Hedge bindweed has large arrow and heart-shaped leaves and, as the name implies, climbs and twines around hedges.

DEWBERRY   X 1 1/8
Rubus trivalis

FAMILY–Rose (*Rosaceae*)
BLOOMS–February to March
HABITAT–Widely distributed all over the state; common

    The delicious fruit appears in April and May,, earlier than the blackberry. Dewberry flowers are solitary and scattered all along the stem; blackberry flowers are in clusters. Which fruit is better is a matter of personal preference. Both plants have thorns, but don't complain: the berries are free.

TEXAS BULL NETTLE   X 3/4
Cnidoscolus texanus

FAMILY–Spurge (*Euphorbiaceae*)
BLOOMS–April to June
HABITAT–Dry pinelands

The flowers of this striking plant are fragrant, but beware of getting too close! The glassy hairs covering the stem and leaves contain a poison and can cause a severe reaction on contact. The hairs break off in the skin and are removed with difficulty. Other names for this plant are large bull nettle and, very appropriately, tread softly.

BEARD-TONGUE   X 3/4
Pentsemon laxiflorus

FAMILY–Snapdragon (*Scrophulariaceae*)
BLOOMS–April to May
HABITAT–Open pinelands, hills, prairies

    Penstemon means five stamens. The fifth stamen is sterile ad has a tuft of hairs; this is the beard-tongue. *Laxiflorus* means loose-flowered, This many-flowered plant is about two feet tall. It is one of several white penstemons found in Louisiana.

LARKSPUR   X 1 1/8
Dephinium virescens

FAMILY–Crowfoot (*Ranunculaceae*)
BLOOMS–April to July
HABITAT–Open woodlands

All parts of the larkspur are poisonous; it jas caused more cattle deaths than any plant but locoweed. *Delphinium* is the ancient Greek word for this plant, from the word for dolphin; probably because the lark's spur resembles the nose or dorsal fin of a dolphin. Elsewhere this flower is referred to as prairie larkspur, but it is not seen in Louisiana's prairies.

FLOWERING DOGWOOD   X 1 1/8
Cornus florida

FAMILY–Dogwood (*Cornaceae*)
BLOOMS–March to April
HABITAT–Widespread, especially in north Louisiana, often near other hardwoods

      The actual flowers are tiny, clustered in the center, and surrounded by four white, petal-like bracts. There is also a pink form. The wood of this small tree is very hard, and has been used for small articles such as spindles, handles and roller skate wheels. Flowering dogwood is the state flower of both Virginia and North Carolina.

RATTLESNAKE-MASTER   X 1 1/8
Eryngium yuccifolium

FAMILY–Parsley (*Apiaceae*)
BLOOMS–May to August
HABITAT–Open pinelands, prairies,, thin , mixed woods

     No master of rattlesnakes, this harmless plant (also known as button snakeroot) was once thought to cure snakebite. *Yuccifolium* is from the yucca-like leaves, which have widely spaced spines on the edges. The parsley family includes the edible plants carrot, celery, dill, fennel, and parsnip, as well as the deadly cicuta and poison hemlock, made famous by the execution of Socrates in ancient Greece.

LADIES' TRESSES   X 1
Spiranthes praecox

FAMILY–Orchid (*Orchidaceae*)
BLOOMS–March to September
HABITAT–Pinelands, wet meadows, low woods

    This species is distinguished from several other ladies' tresses native to Louisiana by the presence of a long lip with green stripes and a wavy edge. The flowers of all ladies' tresses form a spiral around the stem, and are thus named *Spiranthes*. This one is an early bloomer so it is named *praecox*. Another common name is grass-leaved ladies' tresses.

SNOW-ON-THE-MOUNTAIN   X 3/4
Euphorbia bicolor

FAMILY–Spurge (*Euphorbiaceae*)
BLOOMS– August to November
HABITAT–Prairies of wesr Louisiana; sporadically throughout the state

     The actual flowers of this plant are tiny; they are clustered in cup-like structures in the center, and surrounded by long, white-margined, green bracts. This species contains a milky sap which may be poisonous. The spurge family includes many important cultivated plants, including rubber castor bean, cassava and poinsettia. Another for this plant is snow-on-the-prairie.

SPIDER MILKWEED   X 7/8
Asclepias viridis

FAMILY–Milkweed (*Asclepiadaceae*)
BLOOMS–March to September
HABITAT–Prairies, pinelands, fallow fields, ditch banks, fresh marshes

    This genus is named for Asclepias, Greek god of health. The plants were formerely used in medicine. Spider milkweed is a sprawling plant, and the petals of its flowers are spreading; either of these characteristics may have given rise to the common name. *Viridis* means green. It is also known by the common names antelope horn and green milkweed. Like most milkweeds this plant contains a milky sap.

JACK-IN-THE-PULPIT   X 7/8
Arisaema triphyllum

FAMILY–Arum (*Araceae*)
BLOOMS–March to May
HABITAT–Moist woods; widely distributed

The tiny flowers are at the base of a thick stem within the hooded tube; "Jack" is the tip of this stem. The planthas an unserground stem shaped like a turnip; this was cooked and eaten by the Indians, giving us another common name, Indian turnip. If eaten raw, all parts of this plant cause intense burning in the mouth and throat due to acrid crystals.

SPANISH MOSS   X 4
Tillandsia usneoides

FAMILY–Pineapple (*Bromeliaceae*)
BLOOMS–May
HABITAT–Trees, telephone lines; all over the state

Most people are surprised to learn that Spanish moss is a flowering plant, and a member of the pineapple family. It is not a moss (mosses don't flower), nor is it a parasite on trees. The wiry leaves and stem are covered with tiny, silvery scales, which trap moisture and dust particles for the plant's nutrition. The minute, green flower is very inconspicuous.

BLUE-EYED GRASS   X 3/4
Sisyrinchium sp.

FAMILY–Iris (*Iradaceae*)
BLOOMS–March to May
HABITAT–Open grassy areas; widespread

    This is not a grass; it resembles a miniature iris. There are several species of blue-eyed grass in Louisiana, and they are difficult to differentiate, due in part to their natural hybridization. They grow in little clumps and reach a height of six to twelve inches. Another, perhaps more appropriate name for this lovely wildflower is grass iris.

MORNING-GLORY   X 1 1/8
Ipomoea sp.

FAMILY–Morning-glory (*Convolvulaceae*)
BLOOMS–June to Frost
HABITAT–Fence rows, fields, waste places; widely distributed

     These beautiful twining vines, in colors of blue, purple, pink or white, certainly do glorify our mornings as they climb on fence rows, other plants, and even highway signs. Our cultivated sweet potato (*Ipomoea batatas*) is in the same genus as the common morning-glory.

TEXAS BLUEBONNET   X 5/8

Lupinus subcarnosus

FAMILY–Pea (*Fabaceae*)
BLOOMS–March to April
HABITAT–Roadsides; escaped from Texas

Lupines got their names from *lupus*, the latin for wolf, because of the very erroneous belief that they destroyed the fertility of the soil, perhaps wolfing the nutrients. *Lupinus subcarnosus* and all other lupines native to Texas are officially the state flower. *Lupinus texensis* has pointed leaflet tios and is widely planted by the Texas Highway Department.

FIELD SPEEDWELL   X 2 3/8
Veronica agrestis

FAMILY–Snapdragon
BLOOMS–February to May
HABITAT–Lawns, fields, wasrte places

These beautiful but tiny blue and white flowers are escaped exotics, originating in England, where they blanket whole fields (*Agrestis* means growing in the field). The genus is named for St. Veronica, whose handkerchief, according to legend, has the image of the face of Jesus impressed upon it.

PALE LOBELIA   X 1
Lobelia appendiculata

FAMILY–Bluebell (*Campanulaceae*)
BLOOMS–April to June
HABITAT–Prairies, pinelands

    This pale beauty reaches a height of about two feet. Lobelias occur world-wide. Some, on the mountain slopes of East Africa are twelve feet tall. The genus is named for Mathias de l'Obel, a Flemish botanist who was physician to James I of England. The sap of this plant is poisonous.

ELEPHANT'S FOOT   X 1 1/8
Elephantopus tomentosus

FAMILY–Sunflower (*Asteraceae*)
BLOOMS–July to October
HABITAT–Dry, open woods

No part of this pretty woodland plant resembles an elephant's foot (*Elaphantopus*). The unusual flower heads consist of several individual disk flowers with lobes all on one side. The leaves are mostly at the base of the stem, and are densely woolly (*tomentosus*). Other names are tobacco-weed and devil's grandmother.

CHICORY   X 1 1/4
Cichoriu intybus

FAMILY–Sunflower (*Asteraceae*)
BLOOMS–June to October
HABITAT–Fields, roadsides, waste ground

     The long taproot of this plant is roasted, ground and widely used a coffee additive in south Louisiana. The blue flowers are borne along a nearly leafless stem, which reaches a height of six or more feet. The salad vegetable endive is in the same genus. Chicory is an escaped exotic, originating in Europe.

HEDGE-NETTLE   X 1

Stachys floridana

FAMILY–Mint (*Lamiaceae*)
BLOOMS–May to July
HABITAT–Thickets, roadsides; in sandy soil

    These flowers form clusters surrounding the stem at different levels, making an interrupted spike. The hedge-nettle has a square stem characteristic of (but not limited to) the mint family, and reaches a height of about two feet. *Stachys* comes from a Greek word meaning spike.

BLUE STAR   X 5/8
Amsonia tabernaemontana

FAMILY–Dogbane (*Apocynaceae*)
BLOOMS–March to June
HABITAT–Wet areas and ditches in prairies, woodlands, meadows

     This pretty plant stands up to four feet high. The four inch long narrow leaves are dark green and shiny, with a white mid-rib. The genus is named for Charles Amsom, an eighteenth century physician from Virginia. The species is named for Jackob Theodor von Berzabern, a sixteenth centru botanist at Heidelberg, who changed his name to Tabernaemontanus, the Latin form of his name.

SPIDERWORT   X 1/4

Tradescantia hirsutiflora

FAMILY–Spiderwort (*Commelinaceae*)
BLOOMS–March to May
HABITAT–Fry pinewoods, roadsides, waste areas

     This spiderwort, often incorrectly identified as the more northern *Tradescantia Virginia*, is covered allover with short soft hairs, giving it the species name *hirsutiflora*. It is often found in shady areas, especially pine forests. There are also pink and white forms.

MEADOW BEAUTY   X 1
Rhexia mariana

FAMILY–Melastome (*Melastomataceae*)
BLOOMS–April to September
HABITAT–Moist pinelands, meadows, prairies

These perfectly named wildflowers have two unusual features which aid in identification. The eight stamens are bright yellow, with severely curved anthers. The fruit, usually visible with the flower, is shaped like a miniature vase or urn. This species has hairy stem, leaves and urn. The color varies from white to pink to lavender. This flower is also called deer grass.

BUTTERFLY PEA   X 7/8
Clitoria mariana

FAMILY–Pea (*Fabaceae*)
BLOOMS–May to September
HABITAT–Sandy, dry land

    This is an erect plant, but it sometimes climbs on adjoining vegetation. Butterfly pea has the unusual habit of growing upside down, that is with the keel on top and the large standard at the bottom. It has compound leaves in the form of three leaflets.

SALT MATRIMONY VINE   X 7/8
Lycium carolinianum

FAMILY–Nightshade (*Solanaceae*)
BLOOMS–All year
HABITAT–Salt marshes and above the high tide line on the gulf coast

     Why this plant is called matrimony vine is a mystery. The other common name, Christmasberry, refers to the roundish red fruit. This is a woody shrub, with succulent leaves and vine-like branches. It grows to a height of five feet.

NARROW-LEAVED VETCH   X 1/2
Vicia angustifolia

FAMILY–Pea (*Fabaceae*)
BLOOMS–March to June
HABITAT–Roadsides, fields, open areas, waste areas

     This is a European species which h as become established in the above habitats all over the state. The leaf stalks terminate in tendrils, used by the plant for climbing on adjoining vegetation. The scientific name is simply Latin for narrow-leaved vetch. It is also known as common vetch.

NARROW-LEAVED SABATIA   X 1 1/8
Sabatia stellaris

FAMILY–Gentian (*Gentianaceae*)
BLOOMS–June to August
HABITAT–Sandy soil, salt marshes

This lovely wildflower is characterized by very narrow leaves and (usually) a three-pointed yellow spot at the base of each of the five petals. The plant reaches a height of two to three feet. *Stellaris* means starry, probably in reference to the yellow center of the flower.

POLYGALA   X 1 1/8
Polygala mariana

FAMILY–Milkwort (*Polygalaceae*)
BLOOMS–May to October
HABITAT–Sandy soil in pinelands, prairies

     Another name for this plant is Maryland milkwort. *Polygala* means much milk. Plants in the milkwort (not to be confused with the *milkweed*) family were once believed to increase the secretion of milk in cattle grazing them. The attractive flowers of this species are at the tips of slender branches with narrow leaves. The plant is about fifteen inches tall. The roots of most species of *Polygala* smell like candy.

ROUGH SKULLCAP   X 5/8
Scutellaria integrifolia

FAMILY–Mint (*Lamiaceae*)
BLOOMS–March to June
HABITAT–Fields, thin woods; widely distributed

This pretty member of the mint family with an unattractive name does not have the usual mint odor. The leaves, whiuch have a bitter taste, were once used as a treatment for fevers. The entire plant is covered with down. *Scutellaria* is from the Latin word for dish or hump; *integrifolia* means with uncut leaves.

BLAZING STAR   X 1/2
Liatris pycnostachya

FAMILY–Sunflower (*Asteraceae*)
BLOOMS–July to September
HABITAT–Pine woods, prairies

     Standing up to six feet tall, these feathery flowers really dress up our prairies and piney woods in summer. Members of the *Liatris* genus aere difficult to identify, but if you look closely you will see that this species has a densely packed spike (*pycnos*, dense; *stachys*, spike) of flower heads, each containing five or more flowers. The stem is hairy. Another common name is Kansas blazing star.

MIMOSA   X 1 1/4
Mimosa strigillosa

FAMILY–Pea (*Fabaceae*)
BLOOMS–March to September
HABITAT–Roadsides; widespread

The genus *Mimosa* consists largely of trees and shrubs, mostly in the tropics. Our sensitive plant, however, reaches a height of only about three inches. The flowers occur along a siX foot stem, which hugs the ground. The leaves fold together when touched; this sensitivity once prompted people to believe the mimosa had a nervous system. It is also called powder puff and shame plant.

ROSE-PINK   X 1 1/4
Sabatia angularis

FAMILY–Gentian (*Gentianaceae*)
BLOOMS–June to July
HABITAT–Flat pinewoods, dry open woods, prairies

    This attractive, early summer plant takes the form of a small bush, with the branches of the flowers in pairs. The flower has a yellow center with five points, bordered in red. Sabbati was an eighteenth century Italian botanist. The scientific name drops one *b*.

SOUTHERN BLUE FLAG   X 3/8
Iris virginica

FAMILY–Iris (*Iridaceae*)
BLOOMS–March to May
HABITAT–Marshes, swamps, ditches, other rich, wet soil

    This native iris is very showy. The flowers, which are about three inches across, are at the apex of a two to three foot stem. The flower depicted in the French *fleur-de-lis* is an iris. The underground stem, or rhizome, has a long history of medicinal use–under the name orris root. Iris is the state flower of Tennessee.

IRONWEED   X 1 1/8
Vernonia texana

FAMILY–Sunflower (*Asteraceae*)
BLOOMS–June to October
HABITAT–Dry, sandy pinelands, prairies

Ironweeds, so-called because of their hard stems, have only disk flowers, no rays. The flower heads resemble small thistles. This attractive species, also known as Texas ironweed, has very narrow leaves. The genus *Vernonia* is named for the eighteenth century botanist, William Vernon.

SPIDERWORT   X 7/8
Tradescantia occidentalis var. melanthera

FAMILY–Spiderwort (*Commelinaceae*)
BLOOMS–February to July
HABITAT–Sandy soil in open woods in Caddo, Richland, Lafatyette parishes

    Tradescantia ociodentalis (western) is not common in Louisiana; the variety pictured is even less common, found only in three parishes. The distinguishing characteristic is the almost black connection between the anther and the filament (*Melanthera* means black anthers). There are also rose-colored and white flowers, with corresponding brown and yellow anther connectives.

PERSIAN CLOVER   X 2 3/4
Trifolium resupinatum

FAMILY–Pea (*Fabaceae*)
BLOOMS–March to June
HABITAT–Roadsides, waste areas, old fields, lawns

   This beautifully colored clover is widely planted for pasture and hay; it escapes into the above habitats. Like all legumes, Persian clover enriches the soil with nitrogen. *Resputinatum* means bent back, referring to the upside-down position of the individual flowers in the cluster.

IRONWEED   X 1 1/8
Vernonia gigantea

FAMILY–Sunflower (*Asteraceae*)
BLOOMS–August to October
HABITAT–Prairies, pinelands, pastures

This attractive ironweed may be identified by the nine to thirty-two flowers per flower head, and by the cobwebby bracts, which overlap one another like roof shingles. This species grows to a height of seven feet. Ironweeds are unpalatable to livestock, which makes the flowers more noticeable in pastures. Another common name for this plant is tall ironweed.

SPINY THISTLE   X 3/4
Cirsium horridulum

FAMILY–Sunflower (*Asteraceae*)
BLOOMS–March to June
HABITAT–Fields, roadsides, idle land, waste areas; common

 Horrodulim comes from *horridus*, meaning thorny, not horrible.as you probably thought. Called yellow thistle elsewhere, the magenta form is more common in Louisiana. The root is edible when boiled. Little boys break off the flower head and pretend it is a shaving brush.

SWEET PEA   X 1 3/4
Lathyrus hirsutus

FAMILY–Pea (*Fabaceae*)
BLOOMS–April to June
HABITAT–Gardens, roadsides, waste places

Members of the *Lathyrus* genus are called vertchlings. They differ from the vetches (*Vicia*) most noticeably in their larger leaf-segments. This species, which is also known by the name everlasting pea, originated in Europe, as did the cultivated sweet pea, *Lathyrus odorarus*.

HENBIT   X 1 1/4
Lamium amplexicaule

FAMILY–Mint (*Lamiaceae*)
BLOOMS–February to May
HABITAT–Lawns, gardens, fields, waste areas

This oddly shaped little flower seems to appear everywhere in late winter. The scalloped leaves are stalkless near the top of the plant, long-stalked near the bottom. Some sources list henbit as poisonous. Another name for this plant is dead-nettle, from the nettle-like , but stingless leaves. *Lamium* is the Greek name. It is a native of Europe and Asia.

169

BLAZING-STAR   X 1/4
Liatris squarrulosa

FAMILY–Sunflower (*Asteraceae*)
BLOOMS–September to October
HABITAT–Pinelands, prairies

Species of *Liatris* share the common name blazing-star, but *squarrulosa* is more easily distinguished from the others by the twenty to fifty spherical flower heads. The brown-purple bracts under each flower head overlap, resembling shingles on a roof. This plant grows to a height of about three feet.

PURPLE VETCH   X 5/8
Vicia dasycarpa

FAMILY–Pea (*Fabaceae*)
BLOOMS–April to June
HABITAT–Fields, waste areas, roadsides, especially north Louisiana

This is probably the prettiest vetch. A native of Europe, formerly used as a cover crop on this country, it has escaped to our roadsides, beautifying them in spring. The specific name, *dasycarpa* means hairy-fruited, a reference to the plant's seed-pod. Birds eat the seeds. Other names for this plant are smooth vetch and winter vetch.

SMARTWEED   X 1 1/8
Poygonum sp.

FAMILY–Smartweed (*Polygonaceae*)
BLOOMS–May to Frost
HABITAT–Wet areas, fields; widespread

Members of the same family as buckwheat, smartweeds provide food, in the form of seeds, to many different kinds of birds and small mammals. The acrid juice contained in the leaves causes smarting–and occasionally dermatitis–on contact, hence the common name. There are both white and pink flowering species.

WEAK-STEMMED MILKWEED   X 7/8
Asclepias michauxii

FAMILY–Milkweed (*Asclepiadaceae*)
BLOOMS–April to June
HABITAT–Sandy pine flatlands in southeast Louisiana

     This is an endangered species in Louisiana. It is well named because it does not stand erect, buts leans toward the ground. The narrow leaves are in pairs or single, and point away from the ground. The tiny white flowers are tinged in purplish-pink. The species is named for Andre' Michaux (1746-1803), French explorer and plant collector, whence the other common name for this plant: Michaux's milkweed.

193

VERBENA   X 1
Verbena xutha

FAMILY–Vervain (*Verbenaceae*)
BLOOMS–May to September
HABITAT–Fields, edge of woods, waste areas

    Verbena, or, Vervain has a long history in folk medicine, being used for everything from ulcers to epilepsy. It was thought to be effective against enchantment, evil spirits and witchcraft–as shown in this ancient rhyme: "Vervain and dill/ Hinder witches from their will". *Vetbena xutha* is covered with stiff white hairs, giving the plant a hoary appearance.

GLOSSARY

Anther The tip of the stamen; it bears the pollen.

Barren An area of land with few plants.

Bract A reduced or otherwise modified leaf, usually below the flower structure, sometimes resembling petals.

Corm A short, thick, upright underground stem.

Disk Flowers Tiny tubular flowers in the center (disk) of many members of the sunflower family.

Escaped exotic A non-native plant that has escaped from cultivation or from its foreign habitat, and become established as a wildflower.

Filament The threadlike part of the stamen. It supports the anther.

Keel In the pea family, the two lower, united petals.

Legume Any plant in the pea family; also, a type of fruit.

Ovary The swollen base of the pistil. The future seeds develop inside.

Pistil The central female organ of reproduction in a flower, consisting (usually) of a stigma, style and ovary. The fruit develops from this organ.

Ray flowers The petal-like flowers encircling the disk in some members of the sunflower family.

Rhizome A horizontal underground stem, often thickened by food storage.

Rosette A circular cluster of leaves at the base of a plant.

Sepal One of the usually green, leaf-like parts enveloping the flower bud, then later the base of the flower itself. They may be any color and are sometimes mistaken for petal.

Spike Technically, a long cluster of stalkless flowers arranged around a central stem; in this book the term also refers to short-stalked flowers.

Spur A tubular projection from part of a nower.

Stamen The male organ of reproduction in a flower, consisting usually of the anther and the filament.

Standard In the pea family, the uppermost petal; also called banner.

Stigma The often enlarged tip of the pistil. It receives the pollen.

Style That part of the pistil connecting the ovary and the stigma. It is sometimes missing.

Succulent Fleshy and juicy.

Tendril A string-like, usually coiling, modification of a stem or leaf, used for support by climbing plants.

Wings In the pea family, the two side petals.

SOURCES

100 Woody Plants of North Louisiana. Contributions of the Herbarium of Northeast Louisiana University, number 7. Thomas, R. Dale. February, 1988.

Ajilvsgi, Geyata. 1984. *Wildflowers of Texas*. Bryan: Shearer publishing.

Alexander, T.R., R.W. Burnett and H.S. Zim. 1970. *Botany*. New York: Golden Press.

Anderson, A.W. (no publication date) *The Coming of the Flowers*. New York: Farrar, Straus and Young, Inc. (out of print)

Brown, Clair A. 1972. *Wildflowers of Louisiana and Adjoining States*. Baton Rouge: Louisiana State University Press.

Dormon, Caroline. 1958. *Flowers Native to the Deep South*. Baton Rouge: Claitor's Book Store.

Duncan, W.H. and L.E. Foote. 1975. *Wildflowers of the Southeastern United States*. Athens: University of Georgia Press.

Durant, Mary. 1977. *Who Named the Daisy? Who Named the Rose?* Boston: G.K. Hall & Co.

Ellwanger, George H. 1889. *The Garden's Story*. New York: D. Appleton and Company. (out of print)

Grimm, William e. 1966. *How to Recognize Shrubs*. New York: Castle Books.

Harrar, E.S. and J.G. Harrar. 1962. *Guide to Southern Trees*. New York: Dover Publications, Inc.

Kuck, Loraine E. and Richard C. Tongg. 1958. *Hawaiian Flowers & Flowering Trees: a Guide to Tropical & Semitropical Flora*. Rutland, Vermont: Charles E. Tuttle Co.

Leach, Maria, ed. 1972. *Funk & Wagnalls Standard Dictionary of Folklore, Mythology, and Legend*.

New York: Funk & Wagnalls.

Marsh Trail. U.S. Fish & Wildlife Service Pamphlet RF-43640-10. August, 1986.

Martin, Alexander e. 1972. *Weeds*. New York: Golden Press.

Meunscher, W.e. 1962. *Poisonous Plants of the United States*. Revised ed. New York: Macmillan.

Mitchell, Robert T. and H.S. Zim. 1977. *Butterflies and Moths: a Guide to the More Common American Species*. New York: Golden Press.

Morris, William, ed. 1969. *The American Heritage Dictionary of the English Language.* New York: American Heritage Publishing Co., Inc.

Natural Dyes in the United States. U.S. National Museum Bulletin 281. Adrosko, Rita J. 1968.

Notes on Tradescantia (Commelinaceae) v. Tradescantia of Louisiana. Bulletin of the Museum of Life Sciences, Number 4, pages 1-15, L.S.U. Shreveport. MacRoberts, D. T. September 29, 1980.

Orr, Robert T. and Margaret C. Orr. 1974. *Wildflowers of Western America.* New York: Alfred A. Knopf.

Pliny. *Natural History, vol. 6.* trans. W.H.S. Jones. 1951. London: William Heineman, Ltd.

Rickett, H.W. 1968. *Wildflowers of the United States, vol. II, the Southeastern States.* New York: The New York Botanical Garden-McGraw-Hill Book Company.

Skene, Macgregor. 1934. *Wild Flowers.* London: Thomas Nelson and Sons.

Smith, A.W. 1963. *A Gardener's Book of Plant Names.* New York: Harper & Row.

Stefferud, Alfred, ed. 1948. *Grass: The Yearbook of Agriculture, 1948.* Washington, D.C.: United States Dept. of Agriculture.

Tampion, John. 1977. *Dangerous Plants.* New York: Universe Books.

Traupman, John C. 1966. *The New Collegiate Latin & English Dictionary.* New York: Bantam Books, Inc.

Zim, H.S. and A.C. Martin. 1950. *Flowers: a Guide to Familiar American Wildflowers.* New York: Golden Press.

Zim, H.S. and Clarence Cottam. 1951. *Insects: a Guide to Familiar American Insects.* New York: Simon and Schuster.

INDEX OF COMMON NAMES

INDEX OF SCIENTIFIC NAMES